501 Writers One-Liners

A selection of 501amusing one liner's to make you smile and perhaps add a little something *extra* to your next great novel.

QUENTIN COPE

I0426135

MECURIAN BOOKS

https://mecurianbooks.webnode.com

Quentin Cope

COPYRIGHT & DISCLAIMER

CONTENTS

:Introduction:

Introduction

This book of One-Liners is the third in the '501' series. It contains a selection of one line thoughts and ponderings, many of which are amusing and some of which are profound. This offering is aimed mainly at writers and authors as a reminder pad of situations and observations seen through the eyes of someone with a sense of humor, or someone who has taken the trouble to actually sit on that mountain peak ... somewhere, and think!

The format is similar to '501 Writers Useful Phrases' and '501 *More* Writers Useful Phrases' in that the content is divided into ten sections with 50 'one liners' in each section and 51 in the final section.

If this little book does nothing more than bring a smile to your face at three o'clock in the morning, slaving tirelessly over the ending of Chapter Four, after a full day of looking after the kids or holding down a high pressure job for ten hours, then it will have been worth it. However, if only one of the offerings within these pages jogs a memory button, allowing you to construct that searched for finished phrase, then this can only be considered a bonus.

If you like this latest production in the '501' series, then why not catch up with the other two?

Age: This section contains some one-liners relating to age, people's reaction to old age; the pitfalls of youth and the acceptance of middle age. It is meant to be fun and no matter how old you actually are, don't take it all too seriously.

Confucius: Here you will find a section devoted to the sayings of that mythical creature 'Confucius'. If he ever did live, he would have been booked out for his entire existence at dinner parties, but of course, some of his observations on life can be quite profound.

Funny: The epitome of the one liner is the 'funny' one liner. From the 19th Century stages of music-hall to the modern day 'stand-up' comedian, the funny one liner takes pride of place.

Inspirational: Any visit to a motivation seminar, anywhere in the world, can leave you feeling inadequate, with a large bill and several books filled from cover to cover with inspirational one-liners. So forget the bill and simply consult this little collection every day ... you're bound to feel better..!

Love & Emotion: This is a section covering one of the most popular of subjects and all things to do with the emotion of 'Love'. However, surrounding the convictions and feelings of love are many more emotions ... some we are prepared to admit to ... and others not! You'll find many of them here ... in one form or another.

Observations: Many great men and many great

women have spent a lifetime observing nature ... and necessarily ... human nature. Here are some of the results and don't forget ... "A clear conscience is usually the sign of a bad memory"

People: Well people ... this is all about YOU! ... sorry ... it's really all about US! It's about the things we do, the things we shouldn't have done and some things we got away with doing. You will definitely recognize yourself somewhere within the pages of this section.

Relationships: This is the part most can identify with and some have never been able to fathom. Yes, it's that old gnawing problem of relationships and something we all have to take responsibility for. This may bring a knowing smile to more than one readers face.

Sex: A subject close to the heart of many ... and poorly managed by most. There are some great one-liners within these few pages ... and here is something to bear in mind: "Women might be able to fake orgasms ... but men can fake a whole relationship"

Stupidity & Fools: Everyone has a different view of a fool and many of us can remember our most embarrassing moments of complete stupidity. However, if you have conveniently forgotten, here are a few reminders.

******

Hopefully, you the reader … and more importantly, you the writer, will gain something from this latest edition of phrases, sayings and one-liners. It will hopefully make a great reference alongside the other two '501' books in the series, not only at the initial manuscript stage in the production of your next epic novel, but at the tough edit stage where just one small phrase adjustment can make all the difference to flow, pace, excitement and character definition.

Good Luck!

Part 1:

Age

This section contains some one-liners relating to age, people's reaction to old age; the pitfalls of youth and the acceptance of middle age. It is meant to be fun and no matter how old you actually are, don't take it all too seriously.

******

01: Old people love to give good advice; it compensates them for their inability to set a bad example

02: I'd go out with women my age, but there are no women my age

03: Middle age is a time of life when winking at a girl is closing one eye to reality

04: When we're young, we want to change the world... when we're old we want to change the young

05: You know you're getting old when you buy a sexy sheer nightgown and don't know anyone who can see through it

06: The trouble with young writers is that they are all in their sixties

07: A woman is as young as her knees

08: You know you're getting old when you stoop to tie your shoelaces and wonder what else you could do while you're down there

09: The really frightening thing about middle age is that you know you'll grow out of it

10: The best years are the forties; after fifty a man begins to deteriorate, but in the forties he is at the maximum of his villainy

11: Middle age is having a choice between two temptations and you choosing the one that'll get you home earlier

12: Old age is when you know all the answers, but nobody asks you the questions

13: Adolescence is the age between puberty and adultery

14: Age is a very high price to pay for maturity

15: A man's only as old as the woman he feels

16: I'm at an age when my back goes out more than I do

17: Learning to dislike children at an early age saves a lot of expense and aggravation later in life

18: As you get older, the pickings get slimmer, but the people don't

19: When I turned two I was really anxious, because I'd doubled my age in a year, and I thought, if this keeps up, by the time I'm six I'll be ninety

20: People who get nostalgic about childhood were obviously never children

21: Life expectancy would grow by leaps and bounds if green vegetables smelled as good as bacon

22: You still chase women, but only downhill

23: At twenty, we don't care what the world thinks of us; at thirty, we worry about what it's thinking of us; at forty, we discover it isn't thinking about us at all

24: He was either a man of about a hundred and fifty who was rather young for his years, or a man of about a hundred and ten who had been aged by trouble

25: You know you're getting old when work is a lot less fun and fun is a lot more work

26: Middle age is when your broad mind and narrow waist begin to change places

27: Old age is being ready to undertake tasks that youth shirked because they would take too long

28: As a writer, always be nice to those younger than you, because they are the ones who will be writing about you!

29: I can still enjoy sex at 74; I live at 75, so it's no distance

30: Middle age is when you begin to exchange your emotions for symptoms

31: Anyone can get old; all you have to do is live long enough

32: Memorial services are the cocktail parties of the geriatric set

33: There are only two things a child will share willingly – communicable diseases and his mother's age

34: Middle age is that period when a man begins to shed his hair, his teeth, and his illusions

35: Old age is like everything else in life; to make a success of it, you've got to start young

36: The older you get the stronger the wind gets… and it's always in your face

37: The hands on my biological clock are giving me the finger

38: When I was a kid my parents moved a lot, but I always found them

39: If something's old and you're trying to sell it, it's obsolete; if you're trying to buy it, it's a collector's item

40: Middle age is when a woman's hair starts turning from gray to black

41: You're an old-timer if you can remember when setting the world on fire was a figure of speech

42: The comfort of turning 49 is the realization that you are now too old to die young

43: Forty is the old age of youth; fifty is the youth of old age

44: Your modern teenager is not about to listen to advice from an old person, defined as a person who remembers when there was no Velcro

45: The young are always ready to give to those who are older than themselves the full benefits of their inexperience

46: Old age is like learning a new profession; and not one of your own choosing

47: He is so old… when he was in school they didn't teach history!

48: The secret of staying young is to live honestly, eat slowly, and lie about your age

49: Fun is like life insurance; the older you get, the more it costs

50: The man who is a pessimist before 48 knows too much; if he is an optimist after it, he knows too little

Part 2:

Confucius

Here you will find a section devoted to the sayings of that mythical creature 'Confucius'. If he ever did live, he would have been booked out for his entire existence at dinner parties, but of course, some of his observations on life can be quite profound.

******

51: Confucius say... man who have hand in pockets not crazy, just feeling nuts

52: Confucius say... man in bathroom with tool in hand is not necessarily a plumber

53: Confucius say... butcher who back into meat-grinder, get a little behind in his orders

54: Confucius say... creative Chinese chef without utensils can still find ways to stir soup

55: Confucius say... man who take lady on camping trip, have one intent

56: Confucius say... geometry teacher who loses parrot, will have polygon

57: Confucius say… woman who absentmindedly answer door in her nightie is negligent

58: Confucius say… impotent loser is one who can't even get his hopes up

59: Confucius say… Viagra is like Disneyland… a one hour wait for a 2-minute ride

60: Confucius say… happiness is a way station between too little and too much

61: Confucius say… woman who spend much time on bedspring, may get offspring

62: Confucius say… best way to save face, is to keep the lower part of it shut

63: Confucius say… man with chip on shoulder have wood higher up

64: Confucius say… two wrongs not make right, three lefts do

65: Confucius say… single fact can ruin a good argument

66: Confucius say… very first doctor of dermatology, had to start from scratch

67: Confucius say… man who fish in other man's well often catch crabs

68: Confucius say… even a turtle only makes progress when it sticks its neck out

69: Confucius say… egotist is a person more interested in himself, than in me

70: Confucius say… man who is impotent will have Willy-nilly

71: Confucius say… some sex is good… more is better… too much is just about right

72: Confucius say… you see the handwriting on the wall, you're in a public restroom

73: Confucius say… diplomat is a man who can convince his wife that a fur coat will make her look fat

74: Confucius say… tis better to be pissed off than pissed on

75: Confucius say… dry cleaner who is in hurry for a date, will be pressed for time

76: Confucius say… don't let your affection give you an infection – put some protection on that erection

77: Confucius say… dirty hands make your nose itch

78: Confucius say… lovers in triangle not on square

79: Confucius say… man who farts in church sits in own pew

80: Confucius say… honor your personality flaws, for without them, you would have no personality at all

81: Confucius say… he who seeks revenge should remember to dig two graves

82: Confucius say… shotgun wedding is a case of wife or death

83: Confucius say… kiss on the lips is just shopping upstairs for downstairs merchandise

84: Confucius say… woman is the only hunter who uses herself for bait

85: Confucius say… some fisherman catch their fish by the tale

86: Confucius say… definition of a true genius is a nudist with a memory for faces

87: Confucius say… it is not how deep you fish, it is how you wiggle your worm

88: Confucius say… there is no future in writing history books

89: Confucius say… grandchildren are God's reward for not killing your children

90: Confucius say… show off always shown up in showdown

91: Confucius say… at the feast of ego, everyone leaves hungry

92: Confucius say… your strength lies in your continued belief that what you just ate was indeed duck

93: Confucius say… foolish man give wife grand piano, wise man give wife upright organ

94: Confucius say… man who sleep like a baby doesn't have one

95: Confucius say… is impossible to sling mud with clean hands

96: Confucius say… who mix poison ivy with four leaf clover, have rash of good luck

97: Confucius say… do not argue with spouse who is packing your parachute

98: Confucius say… difference between pink and purple, is your grip

99: Confucius say… never cut rope that can be simply untied

100: Confucius say… every teenager should get a high school education… even if they already know everything

QUENTIN COPE

Part 3:

Funny

The epitome of the one liner is the 'funny' one liner. From the 19th Century stages of music-hall to the modern day 'stand-up' comedian, the funny one liner takes pride of place.

******

101: I used to work in a shoe-recycling shop … It was sole-destroying

102: The good thing about lending someone your time machine is that you basically get it back immediately

103: Born free, taxed to death

104: Love may be blind, but marriage is a real eye-opener

105: Judge to prostitute: So when did you realize you were raped? Prostitute, wiping away tears: When the check bounced

106: Why is the man who invests all your money called a broker?

107: Politicians and diapers have one thing in common. They should both be changed regularly, and for the same reason

108: Evening news is where they begin with 'Good evening', and then proceed to tell you why it isn't

109: I didn't fight my way to the top of the food chain to be a vegetarian

110: The shinbone is a device for finding furniture in a dark room

111: Always borrow money from a pessimist. He won't expect it back

112: I intend to live forever. So far, so good

113: My psychiatrist told me I was crazy and I said I want a second opinion. He said okay, you're ugly too

114: Worrying works! 90% of the things I worry about never happen

115: I used to be indecisive but now I'm not so sure

116: With sufficient thrust, pigs fly just fine

117: To be sure of hitting the target, shoot first and call whatever you hit the target

118: If at first you don't succeed, skydiving is not for you!

119: Does this rag smell like chloroform to you?

120: It is hard to understand how a cemetery raised its burial cost and blamed it on the cost of living

121: Impotence is nature's way of saying "No hard feelings"

122: Alcohol is a perfect solvent: It dissolves marriages, families and careers

123: Being a vegetarian is a Native American definition for "lousy hunter"

124: 100,000 sperm and you were the fastest?

125: Stress is when you wake up screaming and you realize you haven't fallen asleep yet

126: What is the most important thing to learn in chemistry? Never lick the spoon

127: No one is listening until you fart

128: What has four legs and an arm? A happy pit bull

129: If you must choose between two evils, pick the one you've never tried before

130: I have to exercise early in the morning before my brain figures out what I'm doing

131: Constipated people don't give a crap

132: If you don't care where you are, then you're not lost

133: Ham and Eggs end up being a day's work for a chicken, a lifetime commitment for a pig

134: Why do women always ask questions that have no correct answers?

135: Why do you need a driver's license to buy liquor when you can't drink and drive?

136: Insanity is defined as doing the same thing over and over again, expecting different results

137: It was love at first sight. Then I took a second look !!

138: Two antennas met on a roof, fell in love and got married. The ceremony wasn't much, but the reception was excellent

139: Never agree to plastic surgery if the doctor's office is full of portraits by Picasso

140: Laugh and the world laughs with you. Snore and you sleep alone

141: All true wisdom is found on T-shirts

142: Depression is merely anger without the enthusiasm

143: Everything is always okay in the end, if it's not okay, then it's not the end

144: Give a jackass an education and you get a smartass

145: I drink to make other people interesting

146: I'm not normally a praying man, but if you're up there, please save me, Superman!

147: If things get any worse, I'll have to ask you to stop helping me

148: If you didn't get caught, did you really do it?

149: Make it idiot proof and someone will make a better idiot

150: Never try to teach a pig to sing. It wastes your time and annoys the pig

Part 4:

Inspirational

Any visit to a motivation seminar, anywhere in the world, can leave you feeling inadequate, with a large bill and several books filled from cover to cover with inspirational one-liners. So forget the bill and simply consult this little collection every day ... you're bound to feel better..!

******

151: Failure is always temporary, only giving up makes it permanent

152: Do a little more every day than you think you can

153: The best way to predict the future is to create it

154: Trust me ... never trust someone who says "trust me"

155: Violence is the refuge of the incompetent

156: A failure is only a failure when you fail to learn

157: It's far better to happily achieve than it is to feel you must achieve in order to be happy

158: Perseverance is the hard work that you do after you get tired of doing the hard work that you already did

159: Even if you're on the right track, you'll get run over if you just sit there

160: The only way of discovering the limits of the possible is to venture a little way past them into the impossible

161: Sometimes we are limited more by attitude than by opportunities

162: Take charge of your attitude. Don't let someone else choose it for you

163: People who say it cannot be done should not interrupt those who are doing it

164: Experience is the child of thought, and thought is the child of action

165: Don't take yourself too seriously, and don't be too serious about not taking yourself too seriously

166: An optimist is a person who sees a green light everywhere. The pessimist sees only the red light. But the truly wise person is color blind

167: Those who cannot change their minds cannot change anything

168: When it's time to die, let us not discover that we have never lived

169: Things turn out best for the people who make the best of the way things turn out

170: The best way to cheer yourself up is to cheer everybody else up

171: The real voyage of discovery consists not in making new landscapes but in having new eyes

172: You can discover more about a person in an hour of play than in a year of conversation

173: Always look at what you have left rather than look at what you have lost

174: Nothing will ever be attempted if all possible objections must first be overcome

175: Optimism means expecting the best, but confidence means knowing how to handle the worst

176: The optimist sees opportunity in every danger; the pessimist sees danger in every opportunity

177: Kites rise highest against the wind; not with it

178: To be a great champion you must believe you are the best. If you're not, pretend you are

179: Keep your face to the sunshine and you cannot see the shadow

180: We are what we repeatedly do. Excellence, therefore, is not an act but a habit

181: Positive thinking won't let you do anything but it will let you do everything better than negative thinking will

182: Successful people ask better questions, and as a result, they get better answers

183: An ounce of action is worth a ton of theory

184: Do not go where the path may lead, go instead where there is no path and leave a trail

185: When you know what you want and you want it badly enough, you'll find a way to get it

186: A goal is not always meant to be reached; it often serves simply as something to aim at

187: As you think, so shall you become

188: Attitudes are contagious, so make sure yours are worth catching

189: Although it's fate that presents the circumstances, how you react depends on your character

190: For every expert there is an equal and opposite expert

191: Be critical of both new ideas and accepted wisdom

192: Try not to be a person of success, but rather a person of virtue

193: Change is not merely necessary to life – it is life

194: Holding on to anger is like grasping a hot coal with the intent of throwing it at someone else and you are always the one who gets burned

195: Our attitude toward life determines life's attitude towards us

196: Words are plentiful but deeds are more precious

197: The best way out is always through

198: Work spares us from three evils: boredom, vice, and need

199: Be not afraid of life. Believe that life is worth living and your belief will help create the fact

200: You cannot raise a man up by calling him down

QUENTIN COPE

Part 5:

Love & Emotion

This is a section covering one of the most popular of subjects and all things to do with the emotion of 'Love'. However, surrounding the convictions and feelings of love are many more emotions … some we are prepared to admit to … and others not! You'll find many of them here … in one form or another.

******

201: A girl must marry for love, and keep on marrying until she finds it

202: Every man is thoroughly happy twice in his life: just after he has met his first love, and just after he has left his last one

203: Loves conquers all things… except poverty and toothache

204: If you can't help out with a little money, at least give a sympathetic groan

205: People say that money is not the key to happiness, but I always figured if you have enough money, you can have a key made

206: What pleases men most is old wine and young women

207: The one you love and the one who loves you are rarely ever the same person

208: A solved problem creates two new problems, and the best prescription for happy living is not to solve any more problems than you have to

209: Happiness is the interval between periods of unhappiness

210: Happiness is a very small desk and a very big wastebasket

211: Love will find a lay

212: A kiss that speaks volumes is seldom a first edition

213: He who laughs ... lasts

214: The penalty for laughing in a courtroom is six months in jail and if it were not for this penalty, the jury would never hear the evidence

215: Inertia accounts for two-thirds of marriages, but love accounts for the other third

216: He who laughs last probably didn't get the joke

217: They laughed when I said I was going to be a comedian; well, they're not laughing now

218: Happiness is nothing more than good health and a bad memory

219: Misery no longer loves company; nowadays it insists on it

220: A person who knows how to laugh at himself will never ceased to be amused

221: We cherish our friends not for their

ability to amuse us, but for ours to amuse them

222: A sense of humor is what makes you laugh at something that would make you sore if it happened to you!

223: Love is the answer ... but while you're waiting for the answer sex raises some pretty good questions

224: Love never dies of starvation, but often of indigestion

225: A dog is the only thing on earth that loves you more than he loves himself

226: To be happy with a woman you must love her a lot and not try to understand her at all

227: A Bride is possibly a woman with a fine prospect of happiness behind her

228: Life does not cease to be funny when people die any more than it ceases to be serious when people laugh

229: A woman is the only thing I am afraid of that I know will not hurt me

230: Love is the delightful interval between meeting a beautiful girl and discovering that she looks like a haddock

231: Life is like an onion; you peel off one layer at a time and sometimes you weep

232: Love is a matter of chemistry; sex is a matter of physics

233: People who say that money can't buy happiness just don't know where to shop

234: One of the indictments of civilizations is that happiness and intelligence are so rarely found in the same person

235: Before I met my husband, I'd never fallen in love, though I'd stepped in it a few times

236: Some of the greatest love affairs I've known have involved one actor – unassisted

237: I moved to New York for my health; I'm paranoid, and New York was the only place where my fears were justified

238: In the arithmetic of love, one plus one equals everything, and two minus one equals nothing

239: Happiness is a small and unworthy goal for something as big and fancy as a whole lifetime, and should be taken in small doses

240: Ways to relieve stress: Make up a language and ask people for directions

241: Cheerfulness is the art of concealing your true feelings

242: God is a comedian playing to an audience too afraid to laugh

243: Modesty in an actor is as fake as passion in a call girl

244: No woman ever falls in love with a man unless she has a better opinion of him than he deserves.

245: Bravery is being the only one who knows you're afraid

246: Love is the triumph of imagination over intelligence

247: Love is so confusing – you tell a girl she looks great and what's the first thing you do?… turn out the lights!

248: One reason I don't drink is that I want to know when I am having a good time

249: The secret of a happy marriage remains a secret

250: Money can't buy happiness; it can, however, rent it

Part 6:

Observations

Many great men and many great women have spent a lifetime observing nature … and necessarily … human nature. Here are some of the results and don't forget … "A clear conscience is usually the sign of a bad memory"

******

251: We live in a society where pizza gets to your house before the police

252: War does not determine who is right – only who is left

253: The early bird might get the worm, but the second mouse gets the cheese

254: A bank is a place that will lend you money, if you can prove that you don't need it

255: Why does someone believe you when you say there are four billion stars, but check when you say the paint is wet?

256: A clear conscience is usually the sign of a bad memory

257: The sole purpose of a child's middle name, is so he can tell when he's really in trouble

258: You do not need a parachute to skydive. You only need a parachute to skydive twice

259: It's not the fall that kills you; it's the sudden stop at the end

260: Never hit a man with glasses. Hit him with a baseball bat

261: When in doubt, mumble

262: A bargain is something you don't need at a price you can't resist

263: Nostalgia isn't what it used to be

264: A TV can insult your intelligence, but nothing rubs it in like a computer

265: A bus is a vehicle that runs twice as fast when you are after it as when you are in it

266: If winning isn't everything why do they keep score?

267: Why is it that most nudists are people you don't want to see naked?

268: Good health is merely the slowest possible rate at which one can die

269: Some mistakes are too much fun to only make once

270: The discipline of writing something down is the first step toward making it happen

271: Hard work never killed anyone but why take the chance?

272: Dogs have masters but cats have staff

273: The probability of someone watching you is proportional to the stupidity of your action

274: For every action, there is a corresponding over-reaction

275: The best way to lie is to tell the truth but carefully edited

276: A conscience is what hurts when all your other parts feel so good

277: Foreign Aid translates as the transfer of money from poor people in rich countries to rich people in poor countries

278: There are no winners in life...only survivors.

279: One tequila, two tequila, three tequila, floor

280: It's so simple to be wise, just think of something stupid to say and then don't say it

281: Alcoholism is the only disease that tries to convince you that you don't have it

282: A fine is a tax for doing wrong whereas a tax is a fine for doing well

283: It's not how good your work is, it's how well you explain it

284: Efficiency is a highly developed form of laziness

285: The farther away the future is, the better it looks

286: Some of us learn from the mistakes of others; the rest of us have to be the others

287: Discretion is being able to raise your eyebrow instead of your voice

288: The trouble with doing something right the first time is that nobody appreciates how difficult it was

289: As one person you cannot change the world, but you can change the world of one person

290: Those who say it can't be done are usually interrupted by others doing it

291: A smile is an inexpensive way to change your looks

292: Failure is the path of least persistence

293: A friend walks in when everyone else walks out

294: Sometimes the best way to figure out who you are is to get to that place where you don't have to be anything else

295: Better to understand little than to misunderstand a lot

296: Honesty is the best policy but insanity is the best defense

297: It takes patience to listen ... it takes skill to pretend you're listening

298: Never tell your problems to anyone ... 20% don't care and the other 80% are glad you have them

299: A Goal is a dream with a deadline

300: Few women admit their age; few men act it

Part 7:

People

Well people … this is all about YOU! … sorry … it's really all about US! It's about the things we do, the things we shouldn't have done and some things we got away with doing. You will definitely recognize yourself somewhere within the pages of this section.

******

301: There are generally two types of people … winners and losers. Winners make it happen; losers let it happen

302: Do not argue with an idiot. He will drag you down to his level and beat you with experience

303: Light travels faster than sound. This is why some people appear bright until you hear them speak

304: We never really grow up; we only learn how to act in public

305: If you think nobody cares if you're alive, try missing a couple of mortgage payments

306: Good girls are bad girls that never get caught

307: Laugh at your problems, everybody else does

308: Never get into fights with ugly people, they have nothing to lose

309: Why do Americans choose from just two people to run for president and 50 for Miss America?

310: Some people cause happiness wherever they go. Others whenever they go

311: Hospitality is making your guests feel like they're at home, even if you wish they were

312: If you are supposed to learn from your mistakes, why do some people have more than one child?

313: When you go into court, you are putting your fate into the hands of people who weren't smart enough to get out of jury duty

314: Children seldom misquote you. In fact, they usually repeat word for word what you shouldn't have said

315: By the time a man realizes that his father was right … he has a son who thinks he's wrong

316: By the time you learn the rules of life, you're too old to play the game

317: Who was the first to see a cow and think "I wonder what will happen if I squeeze these dangly things and drink whatever comes out?"

318: Friends may come and go, but enemies accumulate

319: If you can stay calm while all around you is chaos, then you probably haven't completely understood the situation

320: Experience is what you get when you didn't get what you wanted

321: Why do people keep running over a string a dozen times with their vacuum cleaner, then reach down, pick it up, examine it, then put it down to give their vacuum one more chance?

322: The probability of someone watching you is proportional to the stupidity of your action

323: Do you realize that in about 40 years, we'll have thousands of old ladies running around with tattoos?

324: We are all time travelers moving at the speed of exactly 60 minutes per hour

325: To err is human; to blame it on somebody else shows management potential

326: Materialism is buying things we don't need with money we don't have to impress people that don't matter

327: It matters not whether you win or lose: what matters is whether I win or lose

328: Progress is made by lazy men looking for an easier way to do things

329: See, the problem is that God gives men a brain and a penis, and only enough blood to run one at a time

330: Why do we press harder on a remote control when we know the batteries are getting weak?

331: Why is it called Alcoholics Anonymous when the first thing you do is stand up and say, 'My name is Peter and I am an alcoholic'

332: Every day, man is making bigger and better fool-proof things, and every day, nature is making bigger and better fools.

333: The hardest thing to learn in life is which bridge to cross and which to burn

334: A celebrity is someone who works hard all his life to become known and then wears dark glasses to avoid being recognized

335: Unless you're the lead dog, the view never changes

336: A positive attitude may not solve all your problems, but it will annoy enough people to make it worth the effort

337: The trouble with being punctual is that nobody's there to appreciate it

338: Just about the time when you think you can make ends meet, somebody moves the ends

339: Wise people think all they say, fools say all they think

340: The knack of flying is learning how to throw yourself at the ground and miss

341: Ever notice that people who spend money on beer, cigarettes, and lottery tickets are always complaining about being broke and not feeling well?

342: Sometimes the road less traveled is less traveled for a reason

343: Constipated people don't give a crap

344: You can easily judge the character of a man by how he treats those who can do nothing for him

345: I believe in luck: how else can you explain the success of those you don't like

346: When you stop believing in Santa Claus is when you start getting clothes for Christmas!

347: I've learned that the people you care most about in life are taken from you too soon and all the less important ones just never go away

348: There are two kinds of people who don't say much: those who are quiet and those who talk a lot

349: If you can smile when things go wrong, you have someone in mind to blame

350: I saw a woman wearing a sweat shirt with "Guess" on it...so I said "Implants?"

QUENTIN COPE

Part 8:

Relationships

This is the part most can identify with and some have never been able to fathom. Yes, it's that old gnawing problem of relationships and something we all have to take responsibility for. This may bring a knowing smile to more than one readers face.

******

351: Behind every successful man is his woman, and behind the fall of a successful man is usually another woman.

352: I should've known it wasn't going to work out between my ex-wife and me, because I'm a Libra and she's a bitch.

353: There's a fine line between cuddling and holding someone down so they can't get away.

354: You are such a good friend that if we were on a sinking ship together and there was only one life jacket, I'd miss you heaps and think of you often.

355: Two years ago I married a lovely young virgin, and if that doesn't change soon, I'm going to divorce her.

356: You know your children are growing up when they stop asking you where they came from and refuse to tell you where they're going.

357: The difference between in-laws and outlaws? Outlaws are wanted

358: I married 'Miss Right'... I just didn't know her first name was 'Always'

359: My mother never saw the irony in calling me a son-of-a-bitch.

360: A friend is someone who will help you move, but a good friend is someone who will help you move a dead body.

361: There are two kinds of friends; those who are around when you need them, and those who are around when they need you

362: Sometimes the best helping hand you can give is a good, firm push

363: I'm multi-talented: I can talk and piss you off at the same time

364: True friendship comes when the silence between two people is comfortable

365: To err is human; to blame it on someone else is more human

366: She said she was approaching forty, and I couldn't help wondering from what direction

367: Losing a husband can be hard and in my case it was almost impossible

368: Blowing out another man's flame doesn't make yours shine any brighter, but less

369: You have two choices in life whereby you can stay single and be miserable, or get married and wish you were dead

370: Don't hate me because I'm beautiful, hate me because your boyfriend thinks so

371: The difference between divorce and legal separation is that a legal separation gives a husband time to hide his money

372: I accidently ran into my ex the other day, hit reverse and accidently ran into him again

373: Love is a canvas furnished by nature and embroidered by imagination

374: Even people who are good for nothing can bring smile on your face, when pushed down the stairs

375: Children in the back seats of cars cause accidents, but accidents in the back seats of cars cause children

376: The reason grandchildren and grandparents get along so well is because they have a common "enemy".

377: Friends are like condoms as they are supposed to protect you when things get hard

378: If it's true that we are here to help others, then what exactly are the others here for?

379: When you are arguing with an idiot, make sure the other person isn't doing the same thing

380: Sometimes I wake up grumpy and other times I let her sleep

381: I almost had a psychic girlfriend but she left me before we met

382: Be nice to your kids as they'll choose your nursing home

383: Friends come and go but enemies accumulate

384: Friendship is like money, easier made than kept

385: I didn't say it was your fault, I said I was blaming you

386: I'm trying to see things from your point of view, but I can't get my head that far up your ass

387: If a man tells a woman she's beautiful she'll overlook most of his other lies

388: If you lend someone money and never see that person again, it was probably worth it

389: Marriage is grand, but a divorce is a hundred grand

390: Marriage is an expensive way of getting your laundry done for free

391: When a man steals your wife, there is no better revenge than to let him keep her

392: Family reunions are a time when you come face to face with your family tree, and realize some branches need to be cut

393: The last thing I want to do is hurt you. But it's still on the list

394: My parents only had one argument in forty-five years and it lasted forty-three years

395: The most important thing in a relationship between a man and a woman is that one of them must be good at taking orders

396: Dates are basically where you go out and act like someone you're not until the person likes you enough to be who you actually are

397: If you can't live without me, why aren't you dead already?

398: I went out with a guy who once told me I didn't need to drink to make myself more fun to be around, and I told him, I'm drinking so that you're more fun to be around

399: The guy I fell in love with had an easy going spirit with a fast car; but he wouldn't marry me, so I ended up with you

400: When a man's best friend is his dog, that dog has a problem

Part 9:

Sex

A subject close to the heart of many … and poorly managed by most. There are some great one liner's within these next few pages … and here is something to bear in mind: "Women might be able to fake orgasms … but men can fake a whole relationship"

******

401: Sex is not the answer, sex is the question and "Yes" is the answer.

402: Having sex is like playing bridge; if you don't have a good partner, you'd better have a good hand.

403: If sex is a pain in the ass, then you're doing it wrong

404: Virginity is like a soap bubble, one prick and it is gone

405: The big difference between sex for money and sex for free is that sex for money usually costs a lot less.

406: Children in the dark make accidents, but accidents in the dark make children

407: Does time fly when you're having sex or was it really just one minute?

408: Panties are not best thing on earth, but right next to it.

409: Remember, if you smoke after sex you're doing it too fast

410: Without nipples, breasts would be pointless

411: Men have two emotions: Hungry and Horny. If you see him without an erection, make him a sandwich

412: Women might be able to fake orgasms, but men can fake a whole relationship

413: During sex, my girlfriend always wants to talk to me, and just the other night she called me from a hotel.

414: Silence doesn't mean you're sexual performance left her speechless

415: Why is a bra singular and panties plural?

416: The last time I was inside a woman was when I went to the Statue of Liberty

417: Sex on T.V. can't hurt unless you fall off

418: You have to accept it; your parents HAVE had sex before

419: I love oral sex; it's the phone bill I hate

420: Sex at age 90 is like trying to shoot pool with a rope

421: The sex was so good that even the neighbors had a cigarette

422: A pram … its last year's fun on wheels

423: Genitalia is NOT an Italian airline

424: A man on a date wonders if he'll get lucky but the woman already knows

425: Except for 75% of the women, everyone in the whole world wants to have sex

426: Most women don't know where to look when they're eating a banana

427: Sex is like air; it's not important unless you aren't getting any

428: Software is just like sex, one mistake and you end up giving lifetime support

429: The difference between pornography and erotica is only lighting

430: The web isn't better than sex, but sliced bread is in serious trouble

431: I told her the thing I loved most about her was her mind, because that's what told her to get into bed with me naked.

432: Love is a matter of chemistry; sex is a matter of physics

433: The kiss is a wordless articulation of desire whose object lies in the future, and somewhat to the south

434: My wife wants sex in the back of the car and she wants me to drive

435: My girlfriend always laughs during sex, no matter what she's reading

436: Women will never be equal to men until they can walk down the street with a bald head and a beer gut, and still think they are sexy

437: The trouble with incest is that it gets you involved with relatives

438: I remember the first time I had sex, I kept the receipt

439: How can we possibly use sex to get what we want?... sex *is* what we want!

440: Sex between a man and a woman can be absolutely wonderful, provided you get between the right man and the right woman

441: Marriage is the price men pay for sex and sex is the price women pay for marriage

442: Physics is like sex; sure, it may give some practical results, but that's not why we do it

443: Easy is used to describe a woman who has the sexual morals of a man

444: I'm not a good lover, but at least I'm fast

445: Some people are better imagined in one's bed than found there in the morning

446: Men love to be thought of as funny, except when they're in bed

447: The only thing wrong with being an atheist is that there's nobody to talk to during an orgasm

448: I don't think I'm good in bed; my husband never said anything, but after we made love he'd take a piece of chalk and outline my body

449: Anyone who eats three meals a day should understand why cookbooks outsell sex books three to one

450: I had group sex once, when my wife screwed me in front of the jury

Part 10:

Stupidity & Fools

Everyone has a different view of a fool and many of us can remember our most embarrassing moments of complete stupidity. However, if you have conveniently forgotten, here are a few reminders.

******

451: We are all born ignorant, but one must work hard to remain stupid

452: What he lacks in intelligence, he makes up for in stupidity

453: She is so stupid... she took a blood test and failed

454: She is so stupid... when you said it was chilly outside she went and got a bowl

455: When stupidity is a sufficient explanation, there is no need to have recourse to any other

456: Some folks are wise and some otherwise

457: It is dangerous to be sincere unless you are also stupid

458: Intelligent people, when assembled into an organization, will tend toward collective stupidity

459: If there are no stupid questions, then what kind of questions do stupid people ask?

460: Only two things are infinite, the universe and human stupidity, and I'm not sure about the former

461: In view of the fact that God limited the intelligence of man, it seems unfair that He did not also limit his stupidity

462: Stupid men are often capable of things the clever would not dare to contemplate

463: In politics, stupidity is not a handicap

464: Stupidity has a knack of getting its way

465: I am patient with stupidity but not with those who are proud of it

466: Think of how stupid the average person is, and realize half of them are stupider than that

467: There are four things that hold back human progress – ignorance, stupidity, committees and accountants

468: I don't want to elect anyone stupid enough to want the job

469: Stupidity, if left untreated, is self-correcting

470: Ordinarily he was insane, but he had lucid moments when he was merely stupid

471: Never attribute to malice that which is adequately explained by stupidity

472: She's so stupid… if you give her a penny for her thoughts, you'll get change back

473: You cannot compile a wit out of two half-wits

474: Stupidity got us into this mess, and stupidity will get us out

475: One half of being smart is knowing what you are dumb about

476: Evil and stupidity are randomly distributed

477: There's nothing more dangerous than a resourceful idiot

478: The difference between stupidity and genius is that genius has its limits

479: It is said that if you line up all the cars in the world end to end, someone would be stupid enough to try and pass them

480: The word user is the word used by the computer professional when they mean idiot

481: Talk sense to a fool and he calls you foolish

482: A full tongue and an empty brain are seldom parted

483: There are a good many fools who call me a friend, and also a good many friends who call me a fool

484: A word to the wise ain't necessary, it is the stupid ones who need all the advice

485: Build a system that even a fool can use, and only a fool will want to use it

486: A fool and his money are soon elected

487: People think it must be fun to be a super genius, but they don't realize how hard it is to put up with all the idiots in the world

488: Never let a fool kiss you, or a kiss fool you

489: People with narrow minds usually have broad tongues

490: A fellow who is always declaring he's no fool usually has his suspicions

491: The trouble with the world is that the stupid are cocksure and the intelligent full of doubt

492: A pipe gives a wise man time to think and a fool something to stick in his mouth

493: Most people don't act stupid: it's the real thing!

494: One has fear in front of a goat, in back of a mule, and on every side of a fool

495: Little things affect little minds

496: A man may be stupid and not know it, but not if he is married

497: The first man to compare the cheeks of a young woman to a rose was obviously a poet; the first to repeat it was possibly an idiot

498: Wise men talk because they have something to say; fools, because they have to say something

499: Only a man who has loved a woman of genius can appreciate what happiness there is in loving a fool

500: Every man is a fool for at least five minutes every day; wisdom consists of not exceeding the limit

501: Never attribute to malice that which is adequately explained by stupidity

THE END

MECURIAN BOOKS

https://mecurianbooks.webnode.com

www.quentincope.co.uk